"Reading *Negotiations* is like walking into a boxing match with an indefatigable fighter; you will be struck, and it will hurt. But for all of its ferocity in how it grapples with womanhood, sexuality, assault, and race, this collection is also full of wonder. Of forgiveness. Of tenderness, the like of which, ultimately, delivers the most powerful sucker punch."

—ELIZABETH ACEVEDO, author of *The Poet X*

"The terms of Destiny O. Birdsong's *Negotiations* are scalding and tender. The speaker in this searing debut collection accounts for what has been stolen, what has been given, and what's left. This speaker 'always knows how it looks,' knows the contours of her own 'singular, decadent life,' knows to 'translate each ache/ into inquiry.' Birdsong excavates a national history and her speaker's personal histories, tracks how their intersections and aftermaths wreak havoc in the woman who survives. But Birdsong's *Negotiations* endgame is not simply survival—it aims to flourish."

—DONIKA KELLY, author of *Bestiary*

"Reading *Negotiations* is like grabbing a piece of metal so cold it feels like fire in your palm. . . . A collection that is equal parts pain and power."

—JOSH COOK, Porter Square Books

NEGOTIATIONS

DESTINY O. BIRDSONG

NEGOTIATIONS

poems

TIN HOUSE / Portland, Oregon

Published by Tin House, Portland, Oregon

Distributed by W. W. Norton & Company

Library of Congress Cataloging-in-Publication Data

Names: Birdsong, Destiny O., 1981- author.
Title: Negotiations : poems / Destiny O. Birdsong.
Description: Portland, Oregon : Tin House, [2020]
Identifiers: LCCN 2020015657 | ISBN 9781951142131 (paperback) |
    ISBN 9781951142148 (ebook)
Subjects: LCGFT: Poetry.
Classification: LCC PS3602.I739 N46 2020 | DDC 811/.6—dc23
LC record available at https://lccn.loc.gov/2020015657

First US Edition 2020
Printed in the USA
Interior design by Jakob Vala

www.tinhouse.com

for my mother, who taught me that, sometimes,
leaving is the most important thing you can do

CONTENTS

What moves between us has always moved as metaphor.

—Terrance Hayes

The worst has already happened to us, she said.
What good is metaphor now?

—TJ Jarrett

Negotiations

My pussy is not made of microfiber.
I can't put it on my head to conduct business,
or plan insurrections. It's not big enough
to hide in, dear reader. It's not bulletproof.
It can't be offered to neo-Nazis as a lure
for conversion therapy. That didn't work
for Sally Hemings. I know it can't work for me.

But I could drive to Charlottesville tonight,
sweep blood from its holy soil, like Sally's skirts
dragging the late summer's scorched leaves
across the cobble. Every day, a woman's ghost
catches on something. Sally's last decade
was spent with her children free, but always under
the threat of her high color, the familial ties
revving beneath her skin like V-8
engines. This is why the location
of my anxiety can't be triangulated with hashtags.
The man who ran me off the road while shouting
nigger is somewhere in the trees. And black folks
are always dying in the trees. These are two
of 4,000 recorded reasons I have trouble
driving past trees.

The history of my slavery is a history of fabrics:
osnaburg, wool, denim, linsey, linen.
A few skeins of thread and a handful of blunted
needles. Later, sandwich boards, glitter paint,
a bit of chain draped fashionably across the shoulders.
But not even Sally's calamanco frocks
could have been held together with safety pins.
Someone's puncture-resistant tongue
was already under the collar, flicking
at the whalebone bodice. And it never mattered
if she didn't want to be touched by a nation's needs.
The pickets blister my hands. The crowd
pulses toward me like auction day, salivating
as my unwhite body takes a stage.
In the newsfeed, pink foam and cat ears win the day.
My rage is a ball-gag; my rage is sedated
by the pre-filled syringe of history.
Most of my illnesses are invisible,
and not covered by Medicaid.
I am here because I haven't decided
how I want to die. You keep
inviting me to happy hour
to pick my brain.
The marches are more elaborate,
the plans more brazen:
we should read up on neurotoxins. And it's almost
aphrodisiacal: if you rub against any idea

long enough while wearing a vaginal suit,
it will come to look three-fifths feasible.
But the master's tools are never kind to the hand
rocking the cradle. There are no portraits of Sally,
and no diaries, so I imagine the prick of her tongue
when the forefather asks, smirking, if the tea is poisoned.
When she replies that she is only there to free her children.
When she tells him she never came there to play with him.

i too sing america

but mostly // when it's convenient
when i'm abroad // i fucking love

the constitution // the gall
of the forefathers

still tittering in their // received
pronunciation // sauced up

since whiskey was more
sanitary than water //

& when the woman runs
out of her shoppe on cowley—

where i'm fingering scarves
on the sidewalk—i aim

my accent at her & pull
the trigger // no one

ever says // *nigger* // but we
lock eyes & she know

i know //
what she mean

i learned to count // pound
& pence // after i

kept getting
incorrect // change //

who steals the most?
who steals // what is most

valuable? // i palm
two bottles // of nail lacquer

wander upstairs
for the cookies

& shit // i'm always
hungry // the portions are

always // too small
i need

more dressing // i hear
music coming

from a rucksack // & i dance
in the crosswalk //

at the opposite end
a brown man tells me

my backpack has hiked up
my skirt // i wink & say

soon you won't // give a fuck //
about my body // that's

assimilation // he smiles
says // carefully // have a

nice day // elsewhere //
i'm paying extra

for the excursion
i want // to swim

with the pigs // i need
to touch // something else

that can be offered // for
a small fee

// or slaughtered //
i'm high on hash

browns & all-black
service // i could be dead

in seattle // in baltimore //
nebraska // whachu want

from me? // whachu
got that won't get

me killed?
i ask this

of every // land
i've planted // my feet

on // & loved //
like the forefathers // it tables

the difficult questions //
ocean water slicks

my thighs
i submerge // watch schools

of zebrafish graze
my sister's palms //

sand-softened
like the leather handbag //

she bought in atlanta //
her bracelet // tapped the emblem

like // a prisoner making
music // to the knock

of waves in the hull //
of the women

being dragged upstairs //
the ancestors

never had it so good // maybe
the children // will //

another man // on the beach
grates his stubble // with

a bleached towel
waves a coconut // & says

he can make it strong as
i like // i am carnivorous

& cannibal //
i tip my room key //

& a smile // when i leave
i put all my cards //

in their holsters
i go

like darren //
like jeronimo // no

convictions //
& i

// declare //
nothing.

Harambe for President
(2016 Write-In Ballot)

Koko, whose name meant "firecracker child,"

and whom her handler, Penny, called *self-absorbed,*

would position a toy gorilla's hands with her teeth

to sign "drink." *We are most ourselves*

in the water, says my swim coach. *We only struggle*

to breathe when we remember it can drown us.

If we can forget, we can move forward.

A man I'd like to love tells me this

about our country when the election results come in,

and all of our imaginary children disappear.

My fingers are smaller than Koko's, but still,

I'm bad at touch screens. I check the ballot

twice before pressing Vote. I don't want

to do it wrong. And call me judgmental for hating

every hand who wrote in the name

of a beast. To them, I am living,

but my survival isn't worth nearly as much effort.

Yet, we all take the sticker; we all

brag of our civic duty, gliding home

on a wave of solidarity that feels

like kinship, which is what one Twitter troll

quipped about the little black boy who fell

into Harambe's confused hands: *Just going*

to see his cousins anyway—what's

the fuss? We're dragging each other

through the moat, the space separating

human from feral. Koko never had

babies because she never had a coven,

no sister-mothers to help her groom or forage

for food, save Penny, who taught her her first betrayals:

the signs for "eat" and "browse," the lettuce on which

she was chewing when she picked out a mate

she would never feel comfortable enough to let

touch her—not tenderly, not savagely, not the way

the Great Apes mate, which I do not know

because, contrary to popular opinion,

I am not one. There are many women

whose cheeks and hands they press

into mine. Sometimes they restart my breathing

with their sounds. I may love black women most

because, in our captivity, we hold each other.

Koko liked to chew on the fists of her plastic

babies, then lift one to her breast to suck.

Had she been anywhere else—perhaps eating wild celery

in Angola—she would have been dead years before.

To be confined on one continent is to be hunted

on another. This is why Facebook tells me

I can't leave: *think of the amniotic coffin of the Aegean;*

think of sterilized Ethiopians in Israel.

Quiet as it's kept, had Koko not almost

died and been rescued from a zoo

overstocked with silverbacks and their harvested semen,

she might have been Harambe's grieving mother,

but chance and the votes of white women rule us all.

This is, of course, America, its reddest records

written in the name of their preservation.

Koko's favorite signs were *Koko love* and *Koko good.*

Even her toys could make the plea for water perfectly.

She knew who didn't have the luxury of making mistakes.

Prime Time

In one commercial, the token black mother
sitting with a table of friends at Chuck E. Cheese
doesn't care if the mushrooms in the alfredo
are fresh, and she doesn't need Chef Tony's recipe.
She just wants to know if he's married—*for a friend.*

In another, the lone black girl at the party
has forgotten the relationship between nut allergies
and peanut butter—she just knows her brownies are hitting.
With her stringy weave and badly mimed surprise,
maybe she thought her homegirl's skin too porcelain,
so she fed her something that would stipple it with welts.

(Revenge is always [but never really] a black woman yelling,
flailing and helpless in a room of shuffling feet.)

At a conference, I sip vodka straight and slip
into a green jumpsuit that looks—almost—
like January Jones's at the Emmys.
Donika says: *jewel tones are good for blondes.*
In the lobby, a white man from my cohort holds me
aloft by my elbows, exclaiming: *but you look great!*
as if he'd opened a menu and found
a gluten-free version of desire: me,
wrong-colored and splayed like blood-speckled currency.
My breasts: two overripe apples in a food desert.
My pussy: convenient as an EpiPen—if you keep one around.

Bummer—for my friend, says the mother
when the waitress confirms Chef Tony is, in fact, married.
The choking girl says nothing; neither do I,
but I steady my gaze to meet the man's
benevolent shock, each almost-word
a pollen-flecked stinger hiving my throat:
Trust me, motherfucker. I always know how it looks.

The 400-Meter Heat

I'm most American when I reach for more ketchup
as Shaunae Miller dives across the finish.

I'm blackest when Allyson Felix collapses on the track,
knees up, concealing her last name

and the letters *USA* blistering her chest.
I'm saddest whenever two black women are competing

because I never know who to root for,
and I'm arrogant enough to believe my split loyalty

fails them (which makes me more American again).
This is how it feels to be a problem:

hoping that, when a country's cameras are trained
on your back, and you offer the fruited plain

of your body, it's somehow enough to quench
the parched land where all the mothers keep dying,

each ghost a breath-song trilling in your blood,
and, perhaps, one day, grand mal convulsions—

petechiae like pomegranate seeds jeweling your face.
Every race is a transubstantiation of flesh,

just not to gold, or bronze, or mythical filigree,
but to the fleeting, nameless moment when a foot

finds the chalk line drawn by someone else.
Maybe #magic, or a single, unfortunate tremor

that means nothing until you're dead. Who knows what metals
the gods use to forge victory, which is neither sympathy

nor love, nor more sacred than the foot-fall—
its indiscernible blip magnified for millions

of eyes that only blink when we're winning—
which you too probably missed, although later,

in the dashcam footage, you'll swear to me you saw it.

Emeritus

Only a few degrees separate
　　　　the splotches of color on both our cheeks when I ask
if he's read Olzmann's theory of Guinness and motion,
　　　　Vuong's description of the copper skies of war.
Murillo's conversation with two sparrows.

　　　　I know enough not to ask about women.
He seizes on the birds: *All the greats wrote*
　　　　about birds, but sparrows are biblical and mundane.
Perhaps there should have been kingfishers instead—
　　　　such majesty there; such music! He goes on
about vacations in Sydney and the kookaburras.

　　　　Meanwhile, summer tattoos its ochre fingers
with a latticework of death masks: hammerheads flounder
　　　　on the seabed, fins folding in oil-choked water;
others swim in silver tureens on the coast.

　　　　A glacier the size of Delaware cracks loose
in the Arctic, and in the place where Wilmington
　　　　might be, a polar bear cannibalizes its cub.
Elsewhere, the mother of an unprotected species
　　　　lunges in the eyes of the law, and is euthanized
in front of her four children. Or was it two?

　　　　One grown son? Three and a fetus? And this man
of arts, letters, and no regrets except one—not taking
　　　　the day trip to Canberra—turns to my page:
I don't understand the girl. She does nothing but play
　　　　jacks, drink Kool-Aid with a spoon, and tell her mother
she wants to be a policewoman while the mother

rubs Vaseline *on her legs? There's a message there,*
but I have trouble identifying—well, it doesn't matter.

Read Wordsworth's "We Are Seven," then we can address
what should happen to her together. At this point,

only the Vaseline is interesting. An ethnic thing, yes?
Perhaps, then, a poem from the perspective of the jar?

Elegy for the Man on Highway 52

I hope everything you touch is infested

      the way you think ghettos are.

I hope parasites burrow in you

      and declare forever homes.

I hope someone tells you everything your culture made

      is meaningless: Stonehenge, democracies, and you.

I hope they call you something akin to *nigger* and mean it.

      I hope someone looks at your list of accomplishments

and tells you you failed because you didn't work twice as hard.

      You didn't navigate the structures put in place

by affirmative action and equal pay. You're an embarrassment.

      I hope your children are trying to get over you in therapy.

When they are asked to write down names to burn

      in the cleansing ritual, yours repeats on the paper

like a singular iteration of many crimes.

      But first, I want to go back to your body.

I hope it never feels like a safe place

      to hide. I hope that, at night, blue lights through

the living-room windows glaze sirens onto your skin.

    Even when you spent the whole day at home.

I hope your illnesses are untraceable,

    so you can't blame your mother,

how she dunked your head in her soapy, nose-burning

    dishwater twelve times for wanting to kiss a *nigger*.

I hope, when you think of this, your eyes itch

    and you wonder why you've never been loved.

I want people to defer to hand-waves when asked

    to hold you, or slap you forward for an embrace,

even when you just want to be left alone,

    coasting the highways of the hollows, unassuming as prey.

I want people to go hunting for you on those roads,

    whip their cars in front of you and brake.

I want them to get lucky: no streetlights, no passersby,

    so they do whatever they want to you because they can.

And, if you survive, I want you to spend the rest

    of your life wondering if this was somehow your fault.

After all, your sister reminded you, you're not

      the best driver, and you don't see too good:

a thing she didn't know until she saw it on television.

      I want you to watch documentaries about yourself

and feel like they got the theory of the lone wolf

      all wrong. I want you to be angry because you feel

too inarticulate to correct them—after all,

      you use words like *nigger* in polite company.

Even Spencer and Bannon know better. I want you

      to be nameless for the same reasons I know

their names. I want you to be misunderstood,

      even by the people whose codes you're struggling to speak.

After all, you're a commoner, a wage worker,

      and unfit for the movement. The movement is for *men*.

I want you to suffer because I disagree with your politics.

      Yes, it is reason enough. Yes, I want you to rot,

piece by piece, with everyone you know unwilling

      to enter the room—not because they love you,

but because they just can't take the smell.

    I want them to leave thinking, *it's true: some people*

ain't made like people. Smelled like baboon shit

    in there. I want you to be remembered

as the animal you least resemble. I want people

    in the comments section to be relieved—*just another thug*

off the streets. Now it's safer at night,

    a little quieter on the Fourth of July

without your beer-guzzling and your fireworks

    and your fifty gun-toting cousins. I want you to bleed

uncontrollably and internally—it's cleaner that way.

    And if there are service-issued shells

lodged in your chest, then all the better.

    And if it was your family who first

called for help, then all the better.

    And if your babies are watching, all the better.

The Art of Cannibalism

Lead with   sarcasm   and a woman   you   a black boy

are gifted   with the master's tools   it is only right

that you flaunt them   see how   deftly   you turn

the nib   iambic skeet   for the whites of eyes

then tell them   it's not for them   good cover

story   they like to be

abused   this too   is a fetish   we let them

get away with   because   it's an easy   way

to get off   I too am   culpable   I

have hooked my fingers   into

my pelvis   and read you   read   your woman: "ah!

her mouth!

a welcome aperitif!"

you can   exploit   expectations   if you make her

white   let the   reader live   vicariously   if she's black

or brown   don't forget to mention   the interior

wet of   her mouth   either you are doing

what they are doing

or you are doing   what they want to do

what   they fly   to Brazil for

alleyway   brothels

deals whispered   on the beach   at Ipanema

along with   stories   of riddled bodies

at Candelária   and here   we are

at the body   preferably   some version

of your body   supple and boy   (always boy)

or a childlike man   then kill him

                        again

            this is   whitepage america

we've all done it   shit   I'm doing it now

                        (what you do

            or what you've wanted to do:

hands around   his neck   [bigger]

            your mary   awaits)

            I'm so fucking   selfish

                  tho: I refuse

            to touch   the bessies here

the sacred names   you don't get to say   them

      as you read   this   aloud   laughing

are you done?   aren't you tired?   you and I

we should lie down   in this poem   blunted

and barefaced   we've come

for the evening   though the white girl begs

to give us both head   via text

and the boys   who might   die   for the first time   this summer

are turning

neighborhood corners   in   cramped cars

even with the volume up   we're complicated   and alone

too strange   for this skin

too tight   for the page   which is such

a velveteen space   its long ears   and memory

its   eager   love   for a coughing   fatherless boy to sink into fantasy   see how light

defines   his exposed jaw

like a lamp   in his mother's   living   room

such effortless stew   a reader might never

know   it's a   sickness

it's

a bone   broth

FOUND ART

this publication?   these words?   all mine
fully funded by me   my pain takes its toll

it's a lot of work   a labor   in co-pays & an unrelenting exhaustion
of love   i always try to showcase   how the ventriloquists steal us

black women's voices   when they can to stay relevant
the canon is so   white   this new trend is all about   the Other

i know you published this here first but   i regret it now
you didn't acknowledge it   that good feeling

i hope i've helped *your career*   since i've been vetted   it's OK
the only way we get likes   (that's how they know we're safe)

is when people like you share us i can't—   i can't always
afford promotion myself   so . . .   feel worthy

you're doing such wonderful things   but i want to be an example
please be mindful   of our capacity   for humility

i'm now editing an anthology   of this body's contingent joy
& i could really use you (since   look   proof of purchase

i still own the work)

ode to my body

after Lucille Clifton

you were born in the year of the rooster
& the dismembered   grandmother.

your mama's first christmas alone   trying to guess
how much sugar to put in the pies

& how much can kill.   you were bundled
into the house with the two uncles

sharing one of the bedrooms   & zero baths
(a summer cabin   in another life).

i have treated you like anything i never earned:
every light blazing   fridge wide open

cooling the whole neighborhood.   doors unlocked.
i don't know   how you   survived

the years without sunscreen
or health insurance.   crabs from the first time

i dropped   (nameless
as apple seeds)   into the toilet.

the everclear.   the laxatives.   the black & milds.
you should have happened to a   more

careful woman.   never known
anxiety   or   shame

the 13-hour drive through arkansas   panic
silent as the sleet stickying the windshield.

the lectures taught with a gallon of prep scouring
your insides   the distance to the bathroom tucked

behind one ear   my pride intent
on beating your best time.

if you could speak in languages
other than mucus & loose stools

i would apologize   for this   & other things
just to hear you answer   in a voice not unlike

my own   remind us what we are to each other:
echo   narcissus: both drunk on their own

guile.   both murderous in their
insistence   of love.

you should know   i never looked at you
& blamed your mother   though it is true

i have wished you smaller   with more symmetry
like the stone of a fruit   nestled in the slick flesh

of the world.   in so many ways
i have tried   to discard you.

or i have   cut you in two
with water fasts   nicotine

stretched you to feed
the men   what they wanted

the women   what they could love.
& when you failed   (& i have called

you failure)   whom could i blame?
what wonder is it   that your newest threat

is your own patrol of cells   —house divided
as the country   intent   on stealing

your coverage.   it's alright
that this is the most   epic thing about you.

& alright that   like your ancestors   you might leave
with fewer parts than   those with which you came.

i would promise you   good years
between now   & then   but who   would i

be fooling?   even now   i'm slipping you milk
&   slabs of bread   smeared

with butter.   like all your lovers
i know   how much you can take.

i have come to love   not you
but your   refusal   to be consumed.

i push you up   pill bottles & down stairs.
& every morning   you wrap a thin   new layer

of membrane   around the sac that holds
my heart.   dispatch   a brigade

of cells   with their   sealed warrants
to a host of organs   i hope   i never see

Auto-Immune

Because there are no disposal laws for syringes
  in this state, I keep a bleach jug packed with syringes.

Once, in a dry-lipped fugue, I dropped two pens
  in a new one; now the laundry is blood-fracked with syringes.

Even so, I believe it's clean coming out of the dryer.
  The white-coated vampire states it as fact: syringes

rinse the surgeries away. She's got a house to feed,
  where tiny mouths drool fluid like primed syringes.

I'm not dying yet, but she wants to be sure.
  She asks me to deliver a ransom of syringes.

Labs, she calls them: needle-nosed hounds dispatched
  by her keyboard; she doesn't actually handle syringes.

Instead, she sends me to a different wing. The phlebotomists
  thump the anticoagulant in my syringes:

stop telling people that ain't your hair when you bought it.
  They pull blood but inject beauty—compassionate syringes.

On the drive home, the guardrails look like casket lowerers;
  lane markings, a mortician's stitch; the cars blunt syringes

hunting out home, the vena cava, in which I brine
          a life, my flesh as seasoned by syringes

as my mother's holiday turkeys. I'm suspended between
          every ancestor who lived or treasoned with syringes.

Their ghosts OD in my dreams; riddled with holes,
          they beg me to remember their names. I ask which syringes

could bring them back to life. I awaken
          to track marks under my nose. A new plot of syringes

dampens on the front steps. I am destined to infuse
          survival with meaning, like honey clotting in syringes.

failed avoidance of "the body" in a poem

your therapist wants to know where
     in your body you most feel your anxiety.

you tell her it's in the bones
     behind your face. they have their own

music, like ptolemy's universe,
     and chirp like shuriken

dancing in the road. your therapist says
     you hurt because there are things

you've never been taught to do:
     how to hold yourself in sleep.

how to drive. how to live with men.
     back when you were five—or maybe four—

your father knelt before you for the last
     time, close enough

that you could smell him: a zephyr
     of kool's filter kings and leaving.

he pushed the tricycle toward you, purple and white
        streamers limp as hair on the handlebars.

by the time you mounted that cranium-shaped
        seat, he was gone.

your new goal is to learn to breathe
        through bones, to make flutes of them.

although, in reality, you are much more supple:
        a crooked fold of flesh that comes so quickly

when called. you are the warm-bellied
        animal on the shoulder,

coated in sunscreen and your father's curiosity;
        white-haired possum with his green, green eyes.

you're now the oldest you may ever be.
        you have never before been this afraid.

there are no bodies bound to rush into the room
        when yours becomes a bullet ringing the tiles.

you know all about love's austere and lonely
        offices: checking your stools for blood.

checking your breasts for lumps. checking your neck
        for swelling nodes. checking the locks,

the coffeepot, and all the cracked eyes
        blinking wrath on the kitchen stove.

your own weep against a pillowcase
        you haven't washed, stiff with the

miasma of your hair. you stare
        at pictures of the girlfriend grinning in sunlight.

you feel bad for not being taken with yourself more,
        but your body is all asymptotes and fractals.

your own skin splinters in the dark
        from its dense heat. the pieces

come back together under a halo of prescriptions
        steeping your head in yellow light. sometimes,

while combing your hair, a sliver of cartilage
        lodges in your finger pad. you swallow

the glittering blood and spit out the shard. compared
        to your father, this is not unkind.

somewhere between your skull and the skin
        that swaddles it, all the songs you didn't know

you needed to learn from him crescendo
        and fade to the rhythm of your breathing.

Her

I love the same way I did as a little girl:

best in empty rooms. Babble filling my mouth

and dribbling, my tongue roseate

with the breath of my own name. A caboodle

on the bed—each chamber beating

with tiny glass bottles. Beside it, two

grinning dolls talk of their husbands,

both magicians. One sprouts daisies

from his hands on Fridays, makes Kool-Aid

and cupcakes for dinner, stirring

into them the sweet of the air

with arms pre-crooked for his wife's embrace.

The other is a doctor, a lawyer, a model,

lies rigid on top, never makes demands

and cannot remove her clothes. They shiver loose

after one knock of his polyvinyl lips

and a pair of gigantic hands. I dreamed then:

perfectly sized to fit any room I could

get my fingers into. Everything

in the future looked like Malibu:

palm-treed and sunned—even I was tan,

with spindly legs and conical breasts,

prancing my permanently arched feet

across a bedspread. I see that girl-self

now, holding every object close

enough for her bifocals to transform it

into a life beyond the bounds of Pines Road.

If I could step into that room to show her

what I've become, prove that nothing

would end her, not drive-bys or

the horned puppet who hisses

at scripture in Sunday School, I'd wait

outside the door, letting her peel

her hot pink dreams open like

Now & Laters. She didn't need

anything more than an adult's

undistracted gaze, a tending ear.

And what I want most to tell her—that she was right

in her utter belief she could build a world

and live in it alone; or that she will one day greet

the sag of her imperfect breasts with a murmur

of indulgence, the way she now dissolves

a boll of cotton candy into syrup laced

with her DNA, or sips the remains

of rainbow-speckled milk from pilfered

cups of cereal—I cannot say.

This is a singular, decadent life, a truth

I know would kill her,

or make her murderous in its knowing.

Fable

When T decides he'll put on the grizzly bear

suit already limp with someone else's

sweat, and chase the girls around the fairgrounds,

he's not quite sure what possessed him, or what will—

it just seemed like something to do on an afternoon

already so hot, the quilted and dark interior

felt like a cooling. And what he also found

was a muffling—the shrieks of children and the gurgle

of deep fryers scalding the air were now

garbled as he pranced his claw-heavy feet

on the patty-caked dirt. In the hollowed-out

cadaver of fur, T became hollow

and, soon, rode over the bodies of anyone

who wouldn't get out of his way. First, it was children,

stumbling, dazzled by the melting glitter

of red sno-cones, the golden crackle

of funnel cakes dissolving in their mouths.

Then it was their mothers, indignant at the

anthropomorphized beast who danced a jig

as they scrambled to scoop every pampered bottom

from the ground. The better-salted tongues

threw curses after his wide-legged jaunt

toward the Ferris wheel and the spinning teacups

tilting on steel saucers. But soon, it was teenaged

girls, aloof, absorbed by nail polish, lip balm,

and boys, who were equally oblivious

to paws, upraised, closing in. T ran the girls

because girls are good for running—some were even

track stars at the local high school; the others

he gave a head start, then followed

in quick pursuit, the suit filling with his breath

and aspiration, which made the space

neither colder nor hotter. Somehow, he'd jostled

the head just so, and could see the full

slant of falling bodies slick with flavored

oils and pubescent musk. And just as he did

with the babies, he never stopped—there was no

need when, as he topped one crumpling body,

another girl careened backward in her tall sneakers

a few feet ahead. It was the feel of their torsos

knocking against him; how their spindly limbs

would tangle briefly with his calcified claws,

which were blunt, and far better at bruising

than cutting, and better still at dragging things

a few feet before they fell. One girl lost a strappy

gold sandal: the plastic popped loose from the sole

as she bumped along on her thighs, far enough

to collide into another, whose Mary Jane

slid free from her heel (it was two sizes too large,

but on sale, and so, a steal) and clocked another

full in the face, her earrings flying like horseshoes

tossed by the indifferent boys in a tent

near the rodeo, and landing, as if intended,

onto two foreclaws skimming the air above her head.

Yet another, having already run herself out

of a sensible pair of oxfords, had a cashmere sock

shredded by stiletto nails; and another lost

a proper boll of blueberry cotton candy,

so trampled into the dust it looked as if

a corner of sky had fallen. T made no apologies,

only marveled at the thump of bodies and scatter of charms

that, moments before, were worn either

dearly or nonchalantly, as one does

when one is not aware of how much can be lost

to a whimsical cruel. None were thinking of this, perhaps

not even T, who, had he been accosted, might have been hard-

pressed in the moment to explain where the costume

even came from. No one knew that, beneath, flailed a frail

boy who turned pages for the church organist,

pushed lawn mowers with his small shoulders in summer's dusk.

He was practical as himself, and would grow into

a man with his own petty grievances, stiffening limbs,

and a hopelessness that comes with watching oneself

become a being altogether foreign: old age biting

through his good bones like a beast through birch.

The thought alone is enough to make anyone a monster,

but bears are not monsters, so we don't know

what T has become as he savors the girls' wails

while loping toward trailers lined like dominoes around the carnival.

With a zipper flashing on his back like a blade

no one had the gumption to catch between two fingers

and pull, he watched the houses that had wheeled themselves

into place, void of foundations and, at the moment,

people who would defend them. T thought: *Perfect.*

I can knock them down too if I want. His instincts

were that simple now, and—after the girls—that keen.

a history of dolls

i'm on your shelf
except your shelf is your lap is
a metal railing i'm straddling.
my thighs are plaster-coated
live wires.

& your lap is my great-uncle's lap
& i am ten. & my mother
says she was molested
but she won't say by whom.

he holds me in place
by my belt loops.
my mother makes him
a sandwich in the kitchen.

later she explains
how he would tear open
loaves of bread
if he was hungry.

i tell myself nothing terrible
has happened to me.
today is today. i just
can't tell you *no*.

my lips are puckered
porcelain painted apart.
my tongue a single
brushstroke of pink.

your hanging mouth
huffs a glaze.
your teeth/my thighs
gilded in sunlight's kiln:

a final firing
through an open
window.

Macular Conception

She wrapped all the negative tests in paper towels
and threw them away at the gas station up the street.
Lined the tampons up, one by one, beneath her mattress:
thirty-six. She doesn't want to need them—hopes that,
in the days and weeks of the summer's bilious heat,
she can succeed at failure—at least in the eyes
of the single mothers she knows. Especially her own.

But she wants this. She wants it so badly, she imagines
her skin stretching in sleep. She claws it feverishly,
awakening to trails of crescent-shaped welts on her belly
that resemble a seascape drawn by the hand of a child.
The boy, who has never slept next to a pregnant girl,
has seen these, but he believes they're stretch marks.

The boy believes her, along with her shift manager,
all of her friends, and two of her professors.
But the stash of tampons is dwindling. She can't buy more.
Luckily, the flow is weak—red dabs of spit.
If anyone asks, she can just tell them she's spotting.

Squatting over a restroom seat, she wonders
what her body means to say in this remittance.
The possibilities excite her. Standing, she wills
the unshed blood and refuse to knit a net,
trapping a piece of her lover. This swimming self
nudges against the folds of her endometrium
like a catfish nosing algae from the walls
of an aquarium. She can see it
as clearly as if her womb were made of glass.
She feels its small, open-mouthed kisses stinging
the way the father's does: teeth nicking her tongue.
And the bliss of it—the womb's obedience, and the boy—
brings the rush she never feels. She arches, contracts.

This father, the boy who sleeps next to her, wants to leave
but he won't: she's having a child. Or she will be.
She must be. Beneath yellow traffic lights, she
scratches the sun-visor and makes a wish
that is much more like a prayer: *Please,*
let it count for something that I believe
myself. Because I believe myself.

Spilled Milk

for hoteps

He joked that I was the whitest thing

     he ever put in his mouth, but a king

forgets the taste of his mother before anything

     else. He came to me in the mornings,

after shifts of sitting with the psychopaths:

     waking them up, feeding them fistfuls of meds.

Honey buns and blunts for himself during breaks;

     eyes glazed as if in a prophetic trance.

I am the Bambara proverb for what could happen

     to children conceived in daylight. I'd draw the drapes,

he'd drop his khakis; we made ourselves dark.

     He did it to show me he wasn't afraid,

like when he refused to blink after one of the intakes

     threatened to kill him if he ever dozed off.

Then, there was me, stumbling down the hall of men

     with fathers. He studied *The Great Hymn to the Aten* with his,

described how their fingers skimmed the verses

as his ankh skirted my collarbone, and he entered me

the way the father entered debates

over the exact location of the Garden of Eden:

let's lay out the facts, he would say.

The son and I, we fucked, and later, because

I stopped believing in his household gods,

each of my stomach's valves blistered shut.

Now, he tells me my diseases don't really exist;

they're just European fetishes, like pasteurization.

Such a shame we can't drink each other anymore.

And it was fun: getting pissy on the balcony,

but whenever I'd whisper, *I need, I need,* into a pillow,

he'd stuff the fingers with which he cleaned grown men

into my mouth: *shut up. We do this for fun.*

Can I ever be nineteen again,

with all these years and babies wedged between us,

including the one I made up? He's toasting the groom

in our most recent photos, his teeth as relentless

as Okonkwo's—filed and gleaming. I'm on the dance floor,

scrambling for the bouquet. He sidesteps

the sailing garter, each wingtip a man's

polished back facing east. *You don't know what it's like*

to fall in love with a woman who isn't . . . He'd drift

without finishing, and I'd fade to black,

like the Iranian engineer

his father was too stupid to marry.

Sometimes, an animal asks for its own death

with the sound of a single branch breaking.

I've since learned all the ways he intended to spill me,

then forget my breasts too, those white elephants

wandering in a room of African violets,

a rabble of monarchs rusting their trunks. Still,

I may always want to know where he's headed,

heart cloaked like a dagger. The whole race

in one pocket. One of my tusks

bloodying the other.

Scope

This illness is turning me into a cannibal.
I'm unraveling myself one fistula at a time,
and dreaming of what I can no longer consume:
a scalding dribble of cheese roping my chin;
meat still tinged with pulses of pink.
I'm startled awake by the taste of my own blood
sweetening my throat.
                              Last week I told
a friend about our last time, when you left
the condom unopened on the nightstand—a trick
of the eye, wafer of proof that I have been passed
through by the beast you call yourself;
the camel straddled by the leather dream
of your brain.
                    Why is this poem
turning to you? Because rape
does that to us; in the fitful sleep
of sickness, a breaking fever, it comes
to press its forehead to the cooling cloth.
                              Every night with you
was like this: I had all these children
in me; I carried each one to the bed
you named "Second Coming," built after she left,
when you had only unfinished wood and time.
But you doubted yourself, broke it, built it again.
And each time you told the story was a different
dismantling, a loss of some vital part
in the reassembly:

first it was tenderness; then
I couldn't speak without permission,
then you stopped asking, and I couldn't move at all.
You never wondered why there was no water.
The curd of spit on my belly was an afterthought,
loosed from your throat as if I'd always been
this barren tract of ground you were passing.
                    And this isn't an indictment,
my love—I keep turning over
the same few grains of sand,
comparing memory to definition: say I loved
the ungulate of you; say, every night,
I led each innocence to your bed;
say you kicked them beneath me like pillows; say
you shredded them with your cleft hooves
as I came—if so, then, who gets to choose
the difference between all those nights
and this?
                    I read through all
the doctors' reports. I ask
too many questions before
letting them enter me. I've already
been promised salvation in the guise
of implied consent, a bound wrist. Some days,
while leaning into the oven or into the bowl,
I feel powerful enough to translate each ache
into inquiry. One specialist notes

the tortuosity of my insides, how I take
each thing I consume on a crooked path,
through the length of a twisted course
before it leaves me.

My rapist once said he didn't need anything from me;

there was already a woman, shorter, thicker, dumber,
ensconced in a dopehouse on the side of town
he and I had escaped through magnet programs.
Diplomas. Student debt. A certain dexterity of speech.
She'd spread for him like a pallet whenever he wanted.
Wherever. I boasted I could do the same,
but I didn't mean it. There were papers to grade;
the dog with her spit-wad nose nabbing me
as soon as my feet touched February's floors;
little snatches of sleep, which I stashed between the deliria
of sweating and spreading. Those days, I was thin
as a sheet, I whipped through his doors without a thread
to count and pinned myself to him like clothesline.
I popped onto beds without a wrinkle to my name.
The other one, she had been ripped open before, though not
with his hands. He considered making love to her
her healing. Just the boyfriend stitch until
she could find a suitor. See, he loved me
best because I wasn't broken like her.
But I wasn't broken enough. I liked orgasms.
I thought men his age should eat vegetables and talk
about their feelings. I laughed when I wanted to laugh,
even if it was at him. I liked to work.
There are the lives we barter, and the lives we give.
*There are ways to be chosen, and ways to be tossed
aside*, said my mother. All happen at the hands of men.

Had I known enough to decipher that first lie,
then, perhaps, while watching him rise for a clean towel,
passing my mirrors, marveling at himself,
naked and unblamed, I might have dismantled
the second. I might have considered the fate
of the woman whose mouth I'd stuffed with stigma
and my own will to win him, panting, from her
in a footrace we'd been running since our youth,
bare soles slapping the pavement, the finish line
rusted twine holding everything I wanted
at a respectable distance above her head, out of her grasp.
I might have considered the counterfactual distance
widening (narrowing) between us. I might have saved
at least one of us by calling out the other.

My rapist taught me the proper way to cook bacon

because his father would rave over skillet-blackened

strips, and he wouldn't be his father; not then, not now—

that hulk of a man with his slowly deflating chest,

rummaging for knives the new wife has hidden.

Hoping to remember how to slice an apple,

hoping to remember how to chew it.

You are my knife, my rapist would whisper

to my breasts, to the pillow over my head,

and I was stupid enough to believe I'd split him

open, cure him with sugar, suck salt from the fat,

teach him to love women the way he taught me

to bake flesh: like an afterthought. Like a modest proposal.

But, like I said, he didn't want to be his father,

so I couldn't be his mother, patient as she was,

with her pocketbook loans and her grandbaby running circles

in the makeshift castle of her living room,

while my rapist and I smeared fluids on each other

a few streets away. He'd built that place as a teenager, he said,

after the father left; the girl had a right

to be there whenever she wanted. Daycare was expensive,

and he was saving—for a bigger place—for us.

I was trained to hear *home*, and he knew it,

until the first morning above freezing, when the lights

flickered off, and a man scurried back to his service vehicle

as we watched from the kitchen window, the coil

of rooms cooling around us. He and I

poured pancake batter into Tupperware bowls,

then slammed through his mother's kitchen, still careening

with the joy of surviving the glassy streets.

Buoyed by hot water and warmth, we giggled

and sipped her homemade punch until it reddened

our tongues. Our teeth. Even now, I'm afraid he'll think

I've betrayed him as he reads this, little boy that he was,

always so tired of being ruled by women:

the baby and the mama; the baker, the banker.

I believed when he said judges always take

our word over his. *What a fucking honor,*

I can hear him fuming, flipping these pages

back and forth, looking for his name.

He would tell you there was joy in the beginning,

but we humans, with our windowless ranges—

could I have known the cast of iron in him

would scorch anything left unattended?

Truth is, I never ate so well before

or since. Take that any way you want.

Every morning, when I'd twist the knob,

slide in the meat, I knew what I was doing.

I could have sworn I knew what I was waiting for.

My rapist explained even the water company gets a bill

and I don't know whether it's true, but I'd like to believe it,

that, somewhere, he's lying under a new woman,

and a memory is unhooking from his brain

and traveling loose in his body, like a clot;

like the small, white knot of debris we watched

spinning in a clarifier while touring the plant.

Probably something nasty, he said. *Like a tampon.*

Had to be small enough to clear the first filter.

We get a lot of those. Water comes from the river,

the sewer goes into the river. And there

are homeless people camping near the river.

He had an answer for everything he didn't want to touch

and better answers for the things he did.

I hope that woman is straddling him like

an overpass in winter, and he's learning

concrete can't keep you warm. Or, maybe her body

is the nightstick she jabs into his belly

while she's dumpstering his shit, making room for the gentry.

He's busier now, with all these new condominiums

and their waterfalls chlorinating the lobbies;

the new fire hydrants and drunk drivers—new disasters.

I know he likes this concept of himself:

essential and brave for being the ghost

in the machine of a city that, in a different century,

bought men who looked like him to build sewer lines

and protect forts without blankets or latrines.

For every narrative, there's a series of underground pipes

and someone willing to pay to have them cleaned.

I know what it costs to lay a crime at a black man's feet.

But whenever I turn on the faucet, I'm reminded

whose hands first touched the water before it traveled

into my macaroni noodles or into my hair.

Every night I turn onto my stomach in the bath,

I think of it as a ritual of refusal.

Years after what happened, something lassoed my breath

and dragged it back into me, like a runaway bride

kicking her way over the threshold.

But her return meant I felt everything intensely,

the way water surges through the tap after a freeze

or a disconnection. Like how, one morning,

at my new address, boxes still bruising the cheap

carpet, the walls went silent for no reason.

When I flushed, the room was as quiet

as an absconded hive. I never realized

how the low hum of a phantom current

penetrates everything until someone plunges a key

below street-level, twists a valve into submission.

Minutes later, when the tank started filling again,

I thought, *wrong house?* Maybe someone close by

forgot to mail the check. Or, perhaps,

so many months behind, was letting it be

what it was. I wondered about each neighbor,

then my rapist, then thought, *maybe I should just take*

care of myself, stop filling in the finer details

for the collection agents, who are always trying to calculate

how much he'll pay, and on whose schedule,

almost as if they're the ones he really owes.

hypervigilance

At night, I peel off my skin and hang it inside my closet door. I like the feel of walking around without questions. Sometimes I stand over the pots on the stove, let the heat seep through my breastbone like a balm. Sometimes I sit in front of the box fan and sing into the stream of air. My voice splinters, comes back to me as *chorus*. Sometimes I fly short distances, like from the first-floor landing to the foot of the stairs. I like the way air feels on the exposed flexors in my feet. It reminds me there are many ways to getting free. When I'm done, I crawl into bed, my thoughts billow like open tents against the sky, its luminous grain. Into this he walks, like a husband returning from the fields. But we never talk about the fields. He begins by recounting my day, naming each stuttered word, each moment I held open my hand, awaiting the grasp of another. He cups my face with its lidless eyes and shudders, tells me never to have children. He slips into my skinsuit, performs a pantomime. He laughs about my secrets, remembers my childhood names, which he grinds into the air with his peppered tongue. The flakes fall against my houseless flesh. In the morning, I must return to my skin. Beneath it, I will burn until it is night.

Love Poem with Stockholm

"There is no right way to be a survivor. All of it is ugly."
  —Tafisha A. Edwards

I keep the corners of my vengeance hidden
in daylight, tucked in my palms like origami
cranes. I clench my fists, and I imagine bones
breaking as easily as I crumple the folds.
All day long, I circle this small tank
of a city like a betta, fanning water into
a dun-colored gill, sneaking to the surface
for gasps of air when I think no one is looking.
I am screaming inside my car with the music
pulsing around me—an alibi—when a stranger
clips my bumper in the underground lot.
I'm already inspecting the skid of paint above the tire,
my shrug already knotted at my shoulders
when he emerges with his phone stuck to his face
like a leech. I can hear his wife feeding
him policy numbers, her tinny voice pecking
at the microphone. "Are you OK?
What did you do now? Are you OK?"
When he offers up the scribble of information
like a detective, I parrot, "You're OK. You're OK."

But later that night, when I can unfold my cruel,
I unlatch you from your body and harvest
your skin. It arrives with a thin layer of smog
from the city between us coating the eyelashes;
snow from the mountains—fine as sand—grates the shoulders.

But the light in your eyes is dim:
you're in bedtime mode, your battery at 50%.
And I don't have to ask you to hold me.
I don't ask for anything I take.
But after, I lie on your deboned torso,
passing little nodes of sound about my day.
I describe the music of the door chime
at the bakery, how it rattles in the throat like a bell
when I come and when I go. I show you
how the peeled skin on my knees
and the backs of my thighs is finally healing.
I trace the long scrape on your scalp
where I have dragged you, empty of yourself,
into this hurt museum. I count
each of our artifacts, cracked and twinning.
But you're slumped on your side, and appear to be sleeping.
When I lift your eyelids with my thumbs,
they look like tiny mouths, gaping red.
You're grinding your teeth back and forth like an old
modem: dial, disconnect, redial.
I didn't calculate this well. All I have are limbs,
which I flip, one by one, until you're facing up.
I prop open your mouth with wads of paper.
I carve a labyrinth gill into the space
where your ribs should be, so you too can learn
how to breathe when there is so little water.
And if you were conscious, I would say: *this time?*
This time I got what I was asking for.

Seeing my rapist reminds me there was no Latin word for "volcano,"

for Cave Canem

so when Pliny the Younger described

the magma chamber's collapse, the roil

of quartz and hydrochloric acid storming the bay,

no sensible Roman believed him. Like this city,

where I take my lunch at noon by descending

into the clang of construction zones and traffic,

Pompeii was gentrifying at maddening speed.

Some thought its fall the wrath of Jupiter, or Isis,

displeased with growth after the quake in 62,

which shook every nobleman to his knees

and made every slave a fuller, stomping urine

into garments for a chance at fortune.

I too am skeptical when I see my rapist

at the place where a friend and I dress salads

with oil and sip iced tea jeweled with lemon.

Over her head, our eyes meet, and suddenly

I am a sovereign citizen scoffing

at my body's memory. I train my eye

on anything else: the menu chalked

in slate above our heads like hipster graffiti;

the friend's new necklace. I ask her to tell

the story of each pearl, of the artisan

a continent away, who suggested

hammered silver and baroque stones. This is how

it would happen: our meeting on conflicting business—

mine plebian, his a kind of treason

by proxy. Any good statistician will tell you

the odds are astronomical, but I know better.

We are standing on a 1,000-year floodplain,

where we watched the river glut our city, first

with water, now with the scraps of tall skinnies.

Calculations and politicians often lie.

It's not just my rapist's body and mine, still on the bed

memory makes and remakes—sometimes

consensually. I wonder if he thinks I'm more beautiful now

than disposable. I have a new softness, wrought

from stillness and rage; rounder, but stronger arms;

a face lined with time, terror, and joy;

a cloud of hair that dispersed and grew

again, perhaps more golden than before.

Someone likened its color to precipitate

rising from ore, which may be the best description

for these years, spent in the spark of that first meeting

like struck flint, like the tectonic plates

that crushed Vesuvius into speech. It would be

millennia before such eruptions were called Plinian:

a kind of reckoning for watching the person

who shares your name asphyxiate on ash.

I can recall the heat of my rapist

more than anything; he once boiled my skin,

my blood, my scalp with nothing more

than his phantom limbs rising over me.

Umbrella pine, said Pliny, *I imagine*

because it was thrust upward by the initial blast.

Now, when I come, I call on muscle memory,

the ache and strain of it; how the work makes tears

in tissues that heal only at rest: phreatic explosions

I'd barely heard of, listening with a shudder,

before they happened to me. Now, I believe

the women: the cousins who pointed out neighbors;

the soror who sparred at shadows on the Sigma plot

like a lost gladiator. The other woman.

Last up is myself, the weight of everyone

I questioned hanging like a scutum on my back:

both penance and armor. Listen, I might die

before giving my most accurate account.

Even in this moment, as I insist

on looking away, on the hallucinogenic

qualities of grief, my bones ask me

to recite the date, the current president,

and, finally, my name, which I now understand

as the jump ring on a chain of contiguous fires:

new nomenclature for my arrival

at a truth I must scale each time

before landing the next.

My Therapist Tells Me I Keep Dating My Mother

It's the holidays, and the stretch of I-30 between
Little Rock and Texarkana is a vortex
of clouds, conical spires, black-veined concrete.
Your voice, cutting out over my headset,
is another kind of closing; I'm testing
logarithms here: what questions can I string
between mile markers to make you respond
with the breathless syllables of my name?
When I imagine your mouth baptizing
the collapse of bone at my hip, or the river
below this bridge kissing the rubber song
of my tires, my throat seizes.
The way home is a place where I remember
all the ways I cannot leave myself.
Do you tremble at the memory of your childhood address?
The water that ran rust-colored? The fenceless yards?
Section 8: an infinity of sameness. Did your mother
ever have to tell you good people can live anywhere?
That a woman pregnant with anything will eat dirt
to prepare for the possibilities of two deaths?
Talk to me a little while longer; I'm growing
something the color of my mother's skin in the '80s.
Something like my relief when she'd return
from chopping our Christmas trees in the woods
between our neighborhood and the city. She'd shake them
for birds' nests and water moccasins on the car porch,

then make stir-fry or taco salads and chocolate chip cookies,
and it was the only place I knew where everything
could exist together and make sense,
like her complexion and mine. This was years
before the husbands, before the imprint
of the bathroom cabinet's knob under her eye
like a swelling wreath of purple thistle;
before my brother, throwing tantrums at the airport,
and her breaking down, and me listing toward the gate
in shame as I did every year, to other mothers,
other gods. I think my hands will always be stained
with her blood; maybe there's nothing I can do about that.
But the old days: the layered smell of peppers and pine.
Then one year, of rotting eggs from the heater
that almost killed us. What calm, before we knew
the language of storms—when there was no one
ahead of us to brace for, and no one behind us
we couldn't carry home, dress in light.

Lodestar

You never asked for it, but you sure as hell
    took it: this little space I made for you,
like I once did for the pair of iridescent flip-flops
    my stepsister fished from the synthetics of my
teenage closet, and slipped like tongues into her overnight bag.
    You're the prom kiss I may never have:
my bubble gum, stiff as taffeta, bulging your cheek;
    my silk dress cooling your head like ocean water;
paste-and-glow stars above us—and your lips—agleam.
    We're already in the future. You're a ream of code
humming beneath my pillow; your avatar's aura
    shaming my bedroom's dark like a luna moth.
The broken crescent my body makes as I text
    is a halting question you refuse to answer
in exchanges about long-distance loves and first drafts.
    My critiques are geometries of emojis, each sweating face
a tiny planet strung on a craft wire of hope
    like the planetarium my mother once made for my science fair.
Or maybe it was my sister's. I come from women
    who save their best work for people who won't remember it.
Your published version is identical to the first.
    Your new woman is identical to the last,
and I am fifteen again, in my mother's car.
    She's asking if she should get married again tomorrow,
hair already pinned to her scalp, formaldehyde tips
    floundering in her lap like poison-gummed wings.
After high school, I forgot the number of rings

around Saturn or my moon-clogged heart,
how it ossified the woman I might have become
like a prehistoric insect spinning in amber.
There's enough petrified in me, waiting
for the leer and thaw of your precise language
to begin, like opening strains of *The Twilight Zone*.
And the spiraling contexts of your lines,
testing the gullibility of my sight:
what am I willing to let you tell me I see?
When did you become galaxies under my fingerprints:
my dactyl eye pressed against the screen?
When did I become calculation, theory,
Styrofoam, and wet paint where red dunes, potable water
should be?

the way i listen to you read poems.

only the couplets, and only the shorter ones.
i like to get out of them quickly. i don't like
how warm water feels inside my stomach.
you're playing with old versions of yourself
in my mind. the game is marco polo. you don't
know i'm still learning to swim.
i'm five again, and my cousins call me mannish:
my torso is flat and i am not yet shaped like a woman.
sometimes, the neighboring counties flood, so i
am planning tomorrow's route and wasting time.
earlier tonight, something entered my spirit.
i would call it loneliness, but it's more stiletto.
i watched a movie about a stripper killing her tricks.
i used to believe only certain women could be stupid.
fall in love with pimps and get diseases.
now i'm thankful for wanting only my labia
to stop twitching for hours after i use my hands.
the nurse says the first hepatitis enters through the mouth:
through ill-prepared food, contaminated water.
i am one of the vulnerable populations.
she swabs my arm and tells me to relax.
it's the first illness i've googled in a long time
without fearing i have it, because i already do.
in a way: i take you in small doses, trying to build
immunity. all day long, i'm watching the walls,
trying to see them the way you might see.
i step outside my body like i'm lap-dancing.

i watch you watch me do sit-ups, braid my hair,
brush flakes from my shirt. practice what i'll say
the next time the doctor asks when the symptoms
began. sometimes, briefly, i want to be pregnant.
sometimes, i want you there, amazed and embarrassed.
since it lasts for less than five seconds, it doesn't count.
i use headphones, so your voice doesn't enter my house.
what i mean to say is that neither of us is holy;
we just don't belong together that way,
which is what my mother once told me about women
and your parents. she's older now, and still lonely.
if i asked her again, she might say something different.

love poem that ends at popeyes

it's valentine's day & i hear tires on the slick streets
it is raining a slow   steady rain
the kind that makes me saddest because it seems
endless   & even after   the sky   having forgotten
its big-eyed blue   stands aloof   now   distant
while the sun   mumbling from her side   of the bed
settles   herself   into   a light   doze
i am thinking   of the meal   i won't have to brave
those streets   clamp-thighed   in a passenger seat   to eat
or the flowers i will not have to accept   awkwardly
because flowers are such   strange gifts   why undress
the ground   just to prove   i am special?
we could go to the botanical   gardens   hold hands
smell the smells that come at me   all at once   in a sneeze
or we could pull over on the highway   run through fields
of bonnets   so buckled   with sky
they look   bruised

why has no one ever loved me that way a bonnet
might engorge itself with blue   so much it is a new
color   unnameable   breathless   my loves   hold
their breaths   calculating   they want me   to look
at the food & the flowers & the tiny golden heart
run through   with a golden thread & say thank you thank you
yes   i am wearing silver but now i will wear
only gold & then they expect me to lie down quickly
as if we're children & the fields are bloated with green & it is may

somewhere   the man who doesn't love me   though i wish
i could say the same   is pacing a supermarket floor
his body   a reflection   in the waxed tile
really he is two men   one flesh man   one floor man
& both are moving in a direction away from me
they are picking out fistfuls of roses   or maybe   tulips
maybe assorted flowers with daffodils
& he knows the woman he really loves will dip her nose
into them like a doe & say   thank you   thank you
& she will kiss him with her tacky lips & for the first time
i am not angry that he might lay her down
& ask if he can do   the things he will do

of course she will say yes that is what   you say
when you love someone   right?
it's what i would say   & this time   not
because i've learned what happens
when you say no or when you say   nothing   at all

i am not sad about   whatever she will let him   do
or what she will do to him to make him   smile
make his mouth   form   & his breath catch the emptiness
where a few of his teeth used to be   & make it ache
it's a good ache   when something is missing   & people still love you
i want him to be satisfied   i want him to be happy
also   i want to be happy   we can do that separately
or we can do it   together   we can do it now

94

or we can do it   later   i am a hopeless
romantic   i still make wishes before i blow out candles
last week i asked an oracle   when   not if
i'd find true love   it said *bad reception*   *try*
again girl   & i am trying   i am lying
in bed with my arms around   myself   thinking of what
i will eat when i get hungry   i am willing
to wait for what i want   like when i pull up
to the window & the cashier says it'll take ten minutes
for the spicy dark   & i say yeah yeah that's OK
i still want it   & i pull my car over & i play
my music & i imagine the fried flecks of flour
smothering in the saliva   of my mouth
& oh the biscuits & oh the honey & oh the red beans
in their salty velvet   & i think   this is my own gold
it is not   daffodil gold   it is not supermarket-roses-
gold   it is not a thin-   stringed gold attached to a locket
of expectations   with my face clasped between
two   composite   hearts

but it is good   & it is filling   & it is enough

Long Division

Twenty percent of me wants women—

or maybe just Cardi B. I want us

to fuck up the club after we get dressed

at each other's houses, her jeweled tips

grazing my ribs as she drags the faja

tight beneath my breasts. I want her to call

me *bitch* because I'm taking too long to gel down

my edges, then later, try to fight the bitches

who get too close to me on the dancefloor.

I want us to stumble into the bathroom

arm in arm; for her to thumb straight

the smudged wings of my mascara,

gum cracking against her expensive

teeth, us taking in the breath from

each other's nostrils and the stench

of pissy toilets and bins brimming with pads

rolled tight as sushi. And all this

is to say: I am not ready to speak of her

peacock feather, of the ripple of muscle

coaxing it down her outer thigh, which is

to say: I don't know what I want—but maybe

more than 20 percent will allow.

Sixty-nine percent of me wants men:

I believe every mouth deserves a morsel.

The rest of me just wants a bed alone,

seas of unfucked stitches cool

to the touch, and arms brave enough

to lie open with no expectation of

an embrace. Of that, half is terrified of men:

of the intentions they hide between my fears,

the messages sitting on read, and the easy way

they are speaking to you, then suddenly,

they forget. Though part of me longs

for their forearms, for the way they lift me;

and the laps, broad as my mother's, granite enough

to hold me no matter what size I've become,

no matter the number of cylindrical months

I've spent alone, months the men moisten

and dangle in front of me like squares

between their lips. *You can never finish a whole one*

by yourself anyway, one used to say, lifting the butt,

it's filter pink and warped from my slow drags.

The other half remembers always—and sometimes

with tenderness—my rapist. I see him in passing:

at least twice daily at 11:11—his wish minute.

I see him in razored goatees and in the rhombus

of a Toyota; in the belly, hard as a melon,

which is leading the man who is leading the girl

through a crosswalk littered with brief blushes

of dogwood blossoms blotting the spring rain.

Even now, I wonder if it happened because we were

in love, and if that's true, maybe I should

just get over it. Or call it some other thing:

the need for better safewords. The need

for more boundaries, unrecognized as they are:

little countries with shorelines for skirts

and no kings. Longing is an imprecise

arithmetic, like the medicines calculated

for both histoplasmosis and my survival.

If you sectioned off my heart, it would collapse

like shredded meat cupped between the loaves

of my sesamed lungs, where there is always more breath

than sustenance; still, some nights I sit

alone at the oak table at sunset,

daring my dissection in the cracked reflection

of an empty plate. Others I spend like the Savior's

parabolic bridegroom, who, having passed the sleeping maids

in the courtyard, enters the streets in his

sloshed robes, his kerosene lamp

whittled to a flicker against his chest.

He's calling, "Come. Come. Whosoever,

let them hear; let them come."

ode to my penis

pill crusher // needle flusher

coconut oiler of legs

& the untouched space // beneath

breasts // butcher // baker //

bathwater maker

and when ten thousand fall

at my side // & the phone

goes dry // you are //

my hitching post

of God's // great // grace //

bottle shaker // chalice faker //

everything that ever poisoned us

passed through // so too

have the cures // you raised me

from the dead // sinister digits //

if there's // a right way //

to stroke raw honey from the lioness's

mouth // you stumble // but find it

every time // palm // grazing

her grizzle // how the swarm

quiets // for a moment //

the pupiled areolas

dilate // their vein-

webbed fronds // oh girl // who else

rides me safely // through // Jerusalem

// unsaddled // on her simple back

or massages // my slippery feet with her

whorled hair // i'll never

let your tunic drag //

the ground of want // again //

we'll have each other //

and live // like Lazarus //

unraveling his spool // in the sisters'

stunned silence // the death oils // slipping

from his skin // savior // you track

mirrored light into // my

wilderness //

a little spit //

a little mud //

at the first touch

i saw men // monstrous //

as marching trees //

then // after a second touch //

// just // trees //

Pact

after Tiana Clark

Everyone in Charlie Murphy's
"True Hollywood Stories" is dead,
and I have become the kind of woman
who exclaims: *but they were so young!*
which means I'm still naive enough to believe
there should always be some kind of reason.
But there is no reason why the man Rick James
once called "Darkness" should die from cancer
that warps white blood cells into weapons:
pale shrapnel, as clustered as Rick's ring,
punching holes through Charlie's cackling body.
I'm annoyed that everyone on Facebook is
feeling overwhelmed, when the truth is
we weren't paying attention; and, fuck it, he's gone.
Now, we wish the stories had been longer;
we miss his staccato teeth, how he announced his name,
how quick he was to identify the motherfuckers.

Let me begin again.
I'm finally home from work, watching *Friends.*
Monica and Rachel have lost their apartment
in a lightning round of trivia, where they
couldn't guess what Chandler did for a living.
To thrive unworried about
the livelihoods of people you love
is a kind of privilege.

To live a life unbothered by how
you make money is a kind of privilege.
Shawn Berry, who knew James Byrd till the day
he died, taught me transparency is different
from whiteness, where nothing behind the mask
is clear, like Rachel's window,
wide open on a Saturday morning
above the awny tremor of her head,
which pops up when she hears a black man
greeting the day with his unapologetic song.
And when she asks if he really
has to do that, he just keeps singing. I have become
the kind of woman who watches reruns because
there's no new plot, no new reason
to be alarmed.
We were dragged for loving our lives in '98,
and we are dragged for loving them right now.

Once more, for the people in the back:
today, they pulled Sheila Abdus-Salaam
from the Hudson. She was a judge.
She was black. And she was a woman.
This is how Wikipedia describes her.
No one asks why it took so long
for two of these to first serve
on New York's State Court of Appeals.
None of the men question

whether she jumped.
But a friend texts: *i know ive said*
i hate my life but if something happens
pls dont let them blame it on me.
I am now the kind of woman who holds
other women's obituaries like borrowed money
tucked in the sweaty banks of my breasts, hoping
never to have to fish them out—except, maybe,
after a windfall, and together, we'll remember
hard times vanished, like the children
in Atlanta. Like the girls in D.C. Like indigenous women
everywhere. I tell my friend: *i promise i'll save this message.*
Therapy and caution make this a kind of privilege
as we count and recount the crumpled notes of our lives.
But, this is how we hold each other's space.
This is how we avoid saying goodbye.

Pandemic

after Toni Morrison's "Recitatif"

Don't worry bout they names; we call em

Itty and Bitty cause that's how they came out:

big ole heads and little arms. I told Robert they look

a little bit like E.T. "Or the Crypt Keeper," he said

in that flat way he say everything. "Probably been smoking

since the day they was made." We had told

the nurses we was grandparents, so they let us in NICU

to hold em. They felt light as wadded-up paper

in the bags I throw out when I clean Mr. Mims's office.

But then I felt bad for thinking that, so I whispered into

one of em's ear, "You ain't trash, honey," before

they put her back in the incubator. Robert mighta been right:

Twyla say she stopped using once she knew

it was twins, but we ain't know bout babies at all

till she called us from the hospital room, so

ain't no telling when that was. They didn't

stay in NICU long, though, so I hope Robert

was wrong. First, she say she didn't want em:

the whole time they was there, they wore red bands

on they ankles cause the state thought they was gonna get em,

and I thought of families like the Mims's, with they piles of good

carpet you feel like you sinking in, good kitchen appliances,

and not a lick of love. And the son won't even

speak to em no more cause some counselor

in rehab told him they was "toxic." Marian say

she wish she could do it over again,

but I don't want nobody like her experimenting on my kin.

She ain't never gon care about nothing more than

them purses, wigs, and houses. You know how they are:

got a car for almost every day of the week,

still don't know how to drive. Robert knew

what I was thinking when I asked when

he was gon clean out that junk room once

and for all, so the weekend before they released em,

he called his nephew over and give him twenty bucks

to haul that stuff to the dump. Then he tell me my

best bet is to get most of what they need from Goodwill.

I tried Makeshift Thrift first; one of Robert's nieces

shop there, even though she married rich.

I got two solid cribs and I was looking at this playpen,

then Robert showed up one night with a new one from somewhere.

He threw a pack of sheets on the couch where I

was tryna crochet some blankets and said, "Not everything

gotta be used." That's how he love me. He don't say

much except what's on his mind, but he good, and I love him

cause I ain't always gotta explain.

We ain't poor, but we ain't rich either. Robert

work at the plant and he got good benefits and a pension,

so I worked for the Mims just for mad money till now. The state

kick in a little every month, and somehow got us on WIC

for a couple years—probably cause Twyla still they mama on paper.

State always think you make too much money for help

when you don't, and I didn't want to get the courts involved.

And I don't now. Plus, I tell Robert all the time: she want em,

she can come get em anytime. That's her right.

I just didn't want no more Watsons in the system like that.

We got a couple in Angola and one in Winnfield,

but they got there on they own. I married

into this family young; Robert was old

when we met, so I hold my peace until somebody ask.

Most of em thought I was gon rob him blind anyway, so I just

try to be a good wife and make sure he buy the nephews

Christmas gifts and mind my business. But when I heard

the social worker was coming to the hospital, I ask Twyla

if we could just watch em till she get on her feet.

She say yeah. I made it sound temporary, cause junkie

or no, she a mama; maybe she'll wanna act like one

soon. I know from seeing Danny Mims

how that stuff mess with your head. It affect them

just like it affect us. I caught him on the floor one night, eyes so glassed over I thought I could pop em out

and play marbles. Could barely see his pupils.

I thought he was dead until he tried to talk to me.

I started screaming and ran to get Mrs. Mims.

They took him to the hospital and that was his first time

in rehab. When I told Robert, he got quiet, cause Twyla

his baby sister and he feel like if he hadn't went

to the army, he could have watched her. Her mama say

she started hanging out with that boy up the street and

before she knew it, she was gone. Twyla was Mama Watson's

autumn baby, so she was too old to tell her anything.

She tried to warn her against messin with them folks,

cause that's all they do: make babies, smoke dope, and rob.

But Twyla always wanted to be one of em. Even

as a teenager, she started dressing like em, with all

that makeup, and gunk in her hair. And she didn't run

with ones like the Mims—at least they got money

and a little bit of sense—no, she wanted

the bottom of the barrel and that's exactly what she got.

I hate to say it, but I'm glad her mama dead.

If she can see what's happening now, she too happy

drinking coffee with Jesus in Paradise to care.

At first, I try not to kiss em too much; I didn't want

to get too attached, but they faces started filling out

and sometimes I couldn't catch myself: I kiss they dimples

and wonder who they got em from. And they hair turn

a pretty color after awhile, and they let you comb it

if you pretend like you just playing with em. I'm still

learning how to do their hair though. I can't tell

what they mixed with and Twyla ain't tell us

who they belong to, so I reckon he ain't looking

for em, since neither is she. She don't know we get

a little money. I'm scared she'll think if she take em back,

she'll get it too. It's just a little something.

Itty a little bit behind, and Bitty's eyes

ain't good, but she got a surgery coming up

and we been praying. They almost five now.

Bitty'll talk your head off if you let her.

Robert say even if Twyla come they might

not go. One time, I ask him if we should

go on and file paperwork. He got quiet again,

so I left it alone. I try not to bother him too much

with em. He getting older and I think he thinking about

it too—cause what'll happen if it's just me? But I know

I'll be alright. He play with em a little. They call me

My-My and they call him Mister Robert. They used

to be scared of him, then one day Bitty climb

on top of him while he sleep on the couch, and the other one

followed her cause that's what she do. He woke up

and bounced em a little on his knee, then set em

on the floor, and they kept on playing.

Every morning, Bitty bring her glasses to him

so he can wipe em off, and I don't know where

she get that from. But he put em on her and say,

"Now you ready," and she run get in the car.

And he help her with homework sometimes. Robert good with numbers.

I'm better with words. The kids at school treat em alright,

both of em, even though they in different classes.

It's the older kids in the neighborhood I worry about.

One of em said, "Yo mama a walker," and I thought

they meant streetwalker, but Robert say no.

It's like a zombie. Then Bitty ask what

that is, and he say it's something like a ghost,

and now that's what she wanna be for Halloween.

Itty don't pay nobody no mind. I don't even think

she slow like they say she is; I think she just be

in her own world: she let people in, she keep

people out. And if that's the case, she smarter

than everybody in the house put together.

Still ain't heard from Twyla. A few months after

they was born, she come by to see em.

I don't know how high she was, but if the

look on Robert's face said anything,

she was high enough. She held each of em

like they was somebody else's, giggled

when I told her what they like,

how they were eating and how to make em laugh.

Then she handed em back to me and walked

out, yelling "Bye!" to Robert, who got so mad

he left the room. Next morning, after he

got through drinking his coffee, he set the mug down

in the sink and said, "Don't let her back in here."

I was gon say she didn't mean no harm,

but he turned his back on me quick and

that was that. Didn't matter anyway, cause

we ain't seen her since. The man she brought

neither. They say he into music, moved somewhere

to do it, but I don't know what kind. Any man

don't wanna make a good dollar with his hands

make me wonder. Plus, he was with Twyla and far as

I know, wasn't trying to get her help.

Stuff like that make me suspicious. You can't love somebody

and not want good for em. Itty like singing

and music, though. And she like drums.

One day Robert came home with a set and I bout died.

Racket for hours, but then she just stopped

playing. I was relieved until I started wondering

why, but she wouldn't answer me. Itty talk

when she want to. Robert say leave her alone.

They was big drums. "She can grow back into

em and they'll still fit her," he say. He think

I worry too much. I do. They ain't mine,

but I do.

I meant to say we saw her once. Or it look like

her. On Fourth Street. I went downtown to file

some papers for the girls, and they was with me

cause they always are, and I think we saw her.

She was on the ground, with one of them blankets

on her shoulders, even though it was May. Hair knotted

and snatching in every direction. Woulda been

as hard to comb as the girls'. That's what I was thinking.

We locked eyes for a minute and I hate to say it, but I got scared

she'd say something, or call to the girls, even

though they don't remember her, so I shooed

em past. I don't know if she recognized me,

but it look like she wanted to say something,

so I ran. I didn't tell Robert about it. I know

he'd either hit the roof or it'd break his heart,

and he been slower on his feet lately. I don't want

to bother him. Last night he went out looking

for Halloween costumes. He thought it would be

better to let em pick, but I didn't

want Bitty to be a zombie. I told Robert, "Get her

something else. Something to make her feel

special." He came back with a dress like Dorothy's

and a pair of sparkly red shoes. Bitty didn't know

who she was, but I told her it was somebody

that left home and found family. "Kinda like me!"

She jumped around so much her glasses slipped off

and skidded across the floor. When Robert put em

back on her, she looked at them red shoes close.

"Is these streetwalker shoes?" she asked. And I looked

over at Robert for an answer. He looked at her for a minute,

then got up from the couch, headed to the back of the house.

"I don't know, gal," he told her, "but them shoes

is for little girls who going somewhere."

And he left it at that.

Pickle Goddess

after ASMRTheChew

I'll eat my supplicants, wearing my carpet-green
suit and red lipstick the mothers warned me about.

I do it for the sting of vinegar beneath
my loose crown, for the way it changes

the shape of my mouth. I could be silently
singing hosannas or having orgasms, followed

by the sound of taut skin breaking between
teeth. On the days my joints don't ache, I lift

the gallon from the bottom of the fridge.
The candy lady is dead, so I do the honors:

fish for the big one, fingers puckering
in the chilled brine, the small cut

on my knuckle rinsed alive again with want.
I choose the one with the deep color

on one side, lighter everywhere else. Carve a cross
in the pale butt, stick a Jolly Rancher inside.

I still know how to eat around it, pushing
its winnowing jewel deeper with my tongue.

Back in the day, I'd rub two quarters in my pocket
and sidle down the block, palate already

itching for that first note of garlic
like a money shot. I'm so glad my mama

don't pay for nothing these days, and nobody
is around to tell me I'm smacking too loud.

That no one can see the small gap between
my incisor and canine, where the best

morsels get stuck, and I have to suck them free.
The women in my family raise a hand

to cover that space when they laugh, but I live
for what stings without bitterness, for what

is still edible after months and months
discounted on a shelf. For what salt

serves as sacrament. For false fruit.
For whatever sates me into a raw-mouthed

sleep. For whatever in you is ready to relish
what's left in me unjarred, unlicked—still sweet.

and though the odds say improbable

the black ladies in their printed dresses float
into the deli. tip-tipping across the coat
of grease on the floor. it's still warm in October
so they remove their sunglasses. rub their oiled shoulders
remark: *so cold in here.* one watches purses
while others shimmy to the salad bar. some are nurses
here for conferences. some on lunch breaks
from government jobs downtown. some are flakes.
unemployed. divas. deans. retired. do hair.
edges slick. wand curls crisp in the Freoned air.
they pinch the fainted lettuce onto plates.
they scoop the pitted olives cherries dates
into bowls. the cotton blended florals plaids
prisms paisleys polkas flutter on calves
until they reach their seats. they kiss mustard.
avocado. banana pudding (*really just custard
with mashed-up banana*) from three-ringed fingers.
one sways to the soft-serve machine and lingers
a little too long but returns with a smile:
a swirl cone done up soda-counter style.
every one of them been through something: sit-ins. bombings.
busing. the crack epidemic. Reaganomics.
backdoor abortions. miscarriages. picket signs in front
of the free clinic. and now the white girl with the blunt
bob snatching plates too early. they tap her wrist.
give each other the look. say *it's alright miss
don't worry 'bout us.* my heart liked to stop

when the black ladies nodded their heads and hoops clip-ons drop-
pearls chandeliers gold nickel earrings twirled
above beautiful elbows. not a care in this old world.
republic been crumbled. Black Wall Street crash
'bout a century ago. they leave together. their laughter is brash
and openly secretive (*you bet' not ask*). perfume wafts.
they wave. say *alright girl i'll be seeing you.* one coughs
and i pray it's just the cold air the pollen the pepper
little piece of meat stuck in her throat. the black ladies better
have a blessed day month year life. i mean it the opposite way
they meant it whenever they have to say
it to coworkers. husbands. customers. the demon board
(child i meant deacon). as i leave i touch the table
where they sat. they ain't superhuman. ain't always able
to save the children the men the country or even your silk presses
but whatever they touch. somebody's good god blesses.

Acknowledgments

Grateful acknowledgment is made to the following publications, in which various versions of these poems first appeared or are forthcoming:

The Adroit Journal – "ode to my body"

Boston Review – "Harambe for President (2016 Write-In Ballot)"

Catapult – "and though the odds say improbable"

Cosmonauts Avenue – "i too sing america"

Crab Orchard Review – "Fable"

Electric Literature's *The Commuter* – "Her" and "Prime Time"

Foundry – "the way i listen to you read poems"

Guernica – "Auto-Immune"

harlequin creature – "a history of dolls"

IthacaLit – "My Therapist Tells Me I Keep Dating My Mother"

Kenyon Review – "love poem that ends at popeyes"

Little Patuxent Review – "Macular Conception"

Nashville Scene – "Lodestar"

Northwest Review – "My rapist explained even the water company gets a bill"

PANK – "Elegy for the Man on Highway 52" and "Spilled Milk"

Poetry Northwest – "failed avoidance of 'the body' in a poem"

Poetry Society of America (In Their Own Words) – "Pickle Goddess"

Rattle – "Long Division"

Rockhurst Review – "hypervigilance"

The Shallow Ends – "ode to my penis"

The Southern Quarterly – "The 400-Meter Heat"

Submittable blog – "FOUND ART"

Third Coast – "Negotiations"

Washington Square Review – "Emeritus"

Words Beats & Life: The Global Journal of Hip-Hop Culture – "Pact" "i too sing america" appears in the *Cosmonauts Avenue Anthology*, ed. Aliza Ali Khan, Aba Micah Collins-Sibley, and Bükem Reitmayer (New York: Cosmonauts Avenue, 2019).

"The 400-Meter Heat" appears in *The BreakBeat Poets Vol. 2: Black Girl Magic*, ed. Mahogany L. Browne, Idrissa Simmonds, and Jamila Woods (Chicago: Haymarket Books, 2018).

"The Art of Cannibalism" first appeared in *Cherry Tree: A National Literary Journal @ Washington College 6* (2020).

"FOUND ART" appears in the anthology *Furious Flower: Seeding the Future of African Poetry*, ed. Joanne V. Gabbin and Lauren K. Alleyne (Evanston, IL: Northwestern University Press, 2019).

"ode to my body" appears in *Best New Poets 2018*, ed. Kyle Dargan and Jeb Livingood (Charlottesville: *Meridian* and the University of Virginia Press, 2019).

"a history of dolls" was reprinted in *Town Creek Poetry: 10th Anniversary Issue* (2017).

"My Therapist Tells Me I Keep Dating My Mother" appears in the online anthology *Because We Come from Everything: Cave Canem Poets on the Theme of Migration* (March 2017), and *Bettering American Poetry Vol. 2*, ed. Amy King and jayy dodd et al. (New York: Bettering Books, 2017).

First, thank you, God, for this moment, this opportunity. Thank You for Your timing, which has been both agonizing and divine—I didn't know I needed it, but You did. Thank You for multiple chances, grace, solitude, provision, protection, discernment . . . masturbation! (I had to say it.) Thank You for returning my body to me. Thank You for teaching me how to love it. This book is the narrative of that journey, and I hope I've done right by You in its telling.

Thank You, Jesus, for redemption and hope. Thank You for showing me that, sometimes, you gotta get that healing "out the mud."

I owe so much to my family. My mother, Joan Birdsong, for telling me I could be whatever I wanted, and meaning it. My sister, Angela Birdsong Fellows, for supporting me in so many ways; and my brother, Roy Harris Jr., for laughs and *Martin* marathons. Shout out to the village that raised me: Uncle Carlos and Aunt Anita (prayers up, always!), Aunt Rosetta, Uncle Eric, Mrs. Ruby, and Daphne. And Uncle Mike, Aunt Meri, Aunt Jill, and Mr. Bill, who are gone but never forgotten. Much love to the cousins, play cousins, godsiblings, family friends, and other kinfolks not bound by blood. A very special thank-you to my godmother, Krista Watkins, for your love, and for making sure I'd be a poet by giving me my name. It's the best gift I've ever received.

Writing often feels like a solitary endeavor, but it draws its strength and sustenance from communities. The following folks have laughed with me, cried with me, prayed with me and for me, watched my dog, read and critiqued my work, encouraged me through rejections, and genuinely celebrated my successes. Larrysha Jones (I knew I had to put you first), I could speak none of my most vital languages—literary, emotional, spiritual—without the language you've created with me, and the ways you've let me speak without shame. "Sasha and Marcus," my friend. To Claire Jimenez, The Flyest Umpa: I spent so many years in the same city with you, never knowing the kind of friendship I was missing. Now, you are not only my friend, but a friend to my work, a champion of my dreams, my fierce defender, and a writer I learn new things from every day. I'm lucky to be writing books with you. To Joshua K. Moore: I love you more than all my cabbages! Thank you for marathon conversations, for driving everywhere, for your impeccable taste, and for constantly reminding me of the power of my own words (#churchkidsunite). And Tafisha A. Edwards: you were the first person who gave me permission to call a thing a thing. You saved me. I am honored to be your friend. Donika Kelly, thank you for your gentleness, mentorship, the best hugs, and for the way you say "I love you, Birdsong." You remind me that some things in this world stay gold. Love to Dr. Selena Sanderfer Doss, for black woman brilliance and candor, and for taking care of Gizmo for long stretches when I was away. Additional love to Christina Stoddard and Chris Allison for their kindness, friendship, and loving support. You are both amazing.

I am deeply grateful to the institutions and organizations that have supported my work, and provided me time, space, and resources over the years: Fisk University (and Dr. James Quirin, best history professor ever!); the University of Louisiana at Lafayette; Vanderbilt University's College of Arts and Science, and particularly the Department of English and the MFA Program in Creative Writing. Special thanks to Dr. Kathryn Schwarz and Mark Jarman, who supported my dual degree ambitions; to Kate Daniels, my MFA thesis chair; and Drs. Ifeoma Nwankwo and Hortense Spillers, my dissertation chairs. Many, many biggups to Dr. Nwankwo and The Wisdom Project for employing me these past few years. Thanks to Cave Canem, Callaloo Creative Writing Workshop, Jack Jones Literary Arts, MacDowell, the Ragdale Foundation, and the Tin House Summer Workshop—especially Shane McCrae's group and the THSW 2018 Scholars. Y'all are the best. Thank you, Lance Cleland, for making a way. Love to Katie McDougall and Susannah Felts at The Porch Writers' Collective for always supporting my work; and to the wonderful people at Nashville Public Radio, home of the *Versify* podcast, especially Anita Bugg, Emily Siner, Joshua K. Moore (again), Tony Gonzalez, and Blake Farmer (my favorite hype man). Many thanks to Ciona Rouse, Christine Hall, Matt Johnstone, Kory Wells, Chet Weise, Walker Bass, and Chance Chambers for the wonderful work you've done to create spaces for and celebrate writers in the greater Nashville area.

There are so many people whose hands have held these poems, or held the poems that later became these poems. I appreciate everyone who workshopped with me and/or offered feedback (sometimes in the middle of the night), including Christina Stoddard (again), Lisa Dordal, Meg Wade, Alicia Brandewie, Freya Sachs, Petal K. Samuel, Kaneesha Parsard, Nafissa Thompson-Spires, Nicole A. Spigner, Irène P. Mathieu, Kateema Lee, and Keith S. Wilson.

Thank you, everyone at Tin House, especially Tony Perez and Elizabeth DeMeo. Elizabeth, it's been such a pleasure working with you; you've made this process feel like the dream come true that it really is. Matthew Dickman, your guidance, insight, and kindness have been a godsend. Many thanks to Jakob Vala and Diane Chonette for your hard work on my cover and layout.

I have so much gratitude for the amazing writers who lent their kind words to my book: Jaquira Díaz, Elizabeth Acevedo, Donika Kelly, and Josh Cook. Thank you for reading, for understanding, and for ushering my baby girl into the world with such beautiful, honest language.

Thanks to Kiele Raymond at Thompson Literary, for advocacy and patience.

Lora, thank you for taking this journey with me.

And last, but never least, Tommy "Teebs" Pico: this wouldn't have been possible without you. I tell you all the time, but you are the kind of artist and person I'm desperately trying to be. I hope this is a book you can be proud of.

Notes

The epigraphs are from Terrance Hayes's "Between Practice" and TJ Jarrett's "At the Repast."

"i too sing america": This poem's title is the first line of Langston Hughes's "I, Too." It also contains references to the standup comedy of Bernie Mac: "for the cookies / & shit" comes from Mac's segment on *The Original Kings of Comedy* (dir. Spike Lee: Paramount, 2000). The names "darren" and "jeronimo" refer to Darren Wilson and Jeronimo Yanez, police officers in Ferguson, Missouri, and Falcon Heights, Minnesota, respectively, who murdered black men while on duty.

"Harambe for President (2016 Write-In Ballot)": This title and poem have deep connections to the 2016 U.S. presidential election. According to exit poll surveys, approximately 94 percent of African American women voted for Hillary Rodham Clinton, while 53 percent of white women voted for Donald Trump (www.cnn .com/election/2016/results/exit-polls/national/president). And, although initial estimates were grossly exaggerated, some voters cast write-in ballots for Harambe, a silverback gorilla killed in May 2016 after a boy fell into his habitat at the Cincinnati Zoo (Doug Criss, "No, Harambe didn't get 11,000 votes for president," 10 Nov. 2016, www.cnn.com/2016/11/10/us/harambe-votes-trnd). This poem also references Hanabiko, or "Koko," a western lowland gorilla who was taught sign language and was eventually adopted by Penny Patterson, who met Koko as a doctoral student working at the San Francisco Zoo. Some images from this poem are adapted from the documentary *A Conversation with Koko* (prod. Bonnie Brennan and Robert Visty; narrated by Martin Sheen: PBS, 1999).

"The 400-Meter Heat": The title and first lines of this poem refer to the 400-meter women's heat at the 2016 Rio de Janeiro Olympics. The line "This is how it feels to be a problem" is reminiscent of Du Bois's question, "How does it feel to be a problem," from *The Souls of Black Folk* (Chicago: A. C. McClurg and Co., 1903). The mention of petechiae and grand mal convulsions allude to the death of track and field athlete Florence Griffith Joyner (1959–1998), who passed away in her sleep due to an epileptic seizure. Medical officials initially suspected foul play because of the petechiae, which suggested strangulation, but ultimately determined that she accidentally suffocated during the seizure. The lines "Who knows what metals / the gods use to forge victory, which is neither sympathy, / nor love" are adapted from lines in Kate Chopin's *The Awakening* (New York: Random House, 1899/2000).

"Emeritus": Lines 3–5 reference poems by Matthew Olzmann ("Sir Isaac Newton's First Law of Motion"), Ocean Vuong ("Anaphora as Coping Mechanism"), and John Murillo ("Upon Reading That Eric Dolphy Transcribed Even the Calls of Certain Species of Birds"). The mother mentioned in lines 19–22 refers to several police killings, but particularly that of Charleena Lyles, a pregnant mother of four who was shot to death by police in Seattle, Washington, on 18 June 2017.

"The Art of Cannibalism": "Candelária" refers to the Candelária Massacre in Rio de Janeiro in 1993, during which a group of homeless children were gunned down in front of a church of the same name. Their murderers were a group of men, several of whom were believed to be police officers, who had earlier been heckled by the children. To learn more about this massacre, see the documentary *Bus 174* (Zazen Produções, 2002). The names "Bigger," "Mary," and "Bessie" refer to characters in Richard Wright's *Native Son* (1940).

"ode to my body": This poem's premise—addressing an independently animate self—and select lines ("you were born in the year . . ." and "i would apologize for this & other things") are variants of Lucille Clifton's "the lost baby poem."

"failed avoidance of 'the body' in a poem": This poem was inspired by TJ Jarrett's "How to Hear Music with Your Whole Body." The phrase "love's austere and lonely / offices" is from Hayden's "Those Winter Sundays," while "not being taken with yourself" references Natasha Trethewey's "Genus Narcissus."

"Her": The premise of this poem—the speaker's talking to a younger version of herself and that younger version's potential reaction to an adult stranger—is taken from Marie Howe's poem "The Girl."

"Spilled Milk": The "Bambara proverb" mentioned in line 9 is taken from Maryse Condé's *Segu* (New York: Viking Penguin, 1987, p. 113): "Tradition forbade lovemaking in daylight. It was punished by the birth of an albino child, thought to be a force of evil." Lines throughout this poem, including "I need, I need," "We do this for fun," and "heart cloaked like a dagger," are inspired by lyrics from SZA's songs "Love Galore" (*Ctrl*, Top Dawg, 2017), "The Weekend" (*Ctrl*, Top Dawg, 2017), and "Shattered Ring" (*Z*, Top Dawg, 2014). The last lines of the poem itself allude to the final lines of Mari Evans's poem "Where Have You Gone?"

"Scope": The phrase, "the camel straddled by the leather dream / of your brain" alludes to Maya Angelou's description of rape in *I Know Why the Caged Bird Sings* (New York: Bantam, 1969, p. 65): "The act of rape . . . is a matter of the needle giving because the camel can't."

"My rapist once said he didn't need anything from me": The titles of this sequence, and the general premise of the poems therein (that rapists perform mundane day-to-day actions like the rest of us), are inspired by Tafisha A. Edwards's "Your Rapist is on Paid Administrative Leave."

"My rapist taught me the proper way to cook bacon": The line "to bake flesh: like an afterthought. Like a modest proposal," references Jonathan Swift's essay, "A Modest Proposal for Preventing the Children of Poor People from Being a Burthen to Their Parents or Country, and for Making Them Beneficial to the Publick."

"My rapist explained even the water company gets a bill": Lines in the poem allude to the use of forced labor in the building of the Nashville, Tennessee, underground freshwater pipeline, and the building of Fort Negley, a Union fort erected after the city's capture in 1862. For more information about both events, see Betsy Phillips's "Remembering the 'slaves of the Corporation'—the people the city of Nashville bought and owned," *Nashville Scene*, 13 Feb. 2014 (www .nashvillescene.com/news/pith-in-the-wind/article/13052558/remembering-the-slaves-of-the-corporation-the-people-the-city-of-nashville-bought-and-owned), and Nina Cardona's "The Complicated History of Nashville's Fort Negley," Nashville Public Radio, 15 Sept. 2017 (www.nashvillepublicradio .org/post/complicated-history-nashvilles-fort-negley#stream/0).

"hypervigilance": The concept of this poem is based on the *soucouyant,* a vampiric witch who, in Caribbean folklore, escapes her skin at night in search of victims. In Edwidge Danticat's *Breath, Eyes, Memory* (1994), however, the protagonist, Sophie Caco, hears cane cutters singing about a woman who flies without her skin at night, but is killed when, one morning, she cannot put it back on because her husband has peppered it.

"Love Poem with Stockholm": The epigraph is taken from a conversation with the poet Tafisha A. Edwards, and her recommendation that I read Jan Beatty's poem "Shooter" was instrumental to my revision of this poem.

"Seeing my rapist reminds me there was no Latin word for 'volcano'": Details about the rebuilding and destruction of Pompeii, the eruption of Mt. Vesuvius, and Pliny's unbelieved account of the events (including the death of his uncle, Pliny the Elder) are adapted from two documentaries: *Pompeii: The Last Day* (dir. Peter Nicholson; prod. Ailsa Orr; narrated by Alisdair Simpson, F. Murray Abraham: BBC, 2003), and *The Private Lives of Pompeii* (www.youtube .com/watch?v=rlII5C0oV-s). Pliny's words are culled and quoted from "The Destruction of Pompeii, 79 AD" (www.eyewitnesstohistory.com/pompeii.htm) and "The A.D. 79 Eruption at Mt. Vesuvius" (www.igppweb.ucsd.edu/~gabi/ sio15/lectures/volcanoes/pliny.html). The final lines pay homage to the final lines of Adrienne Rich's "From a Survivor."

"Long Division": The last seven lines of this poem marry two of Jesus's parables: the parable of the ten bridesmaids (Matthew 25:1–12), and the parable of the king's feast (Matthew 22:1–14). The final line itself is a variation of Revelations 22:17.

"ode to my penis": "and when ten thousand fall // at my side //" comes from Psalms 91:7; "if there's // a right way // to stroke raw honey from the lioness's / mouth //" comes from the story of Samson and the lion (Judges 14) as well as a lyric from Johnny Gill's "Rub You the Right Way" (*Johnny Gill*, Motown, 1990); "the pupiled areolas / dilate // their vein- / webbed fronds // oh girl // who else / rides me safely // through // Jerusalem" references Jesus's arrival to the city shortly before his death (Matthew 21:1–11, Mark 11:1–11, Luke 19:28–44, and John 12:12–19); "or massages // my slippery feet with her / whorled hair //" alludes to the story of a woman who washes Jesus's feet with her hair (Luke 7:36–50, John 11:1–2, 12:1–8); "like Lazarus // unraveling his spool // in the sisters' / stunned silence // the death oils // slipping / from his skin //" references the resurrection of Lazarus (John 11:1–44); and finally, "a little spit // a little mud // at the first touch / i saw men // monstrous // as marching trees //" refers to two of Jesus's healings of blind men (John 9, Mark 8:22–26).

"Pact": This poem's structure and content are influenced by Tiana Clark's "The Frequency of Goodnight," Terrance Hayes's "The Same City," and Philip Levine's "Let Me Begin Again." The last lines echo Clark's final lines. This poem also references various episodes of *Chappelle's Show* (Comedy Central, 2003–2006), and season 4, episodes 12 and 19 of *Friends*: "The One With the Embryos," and "The One With All the Haste" (first aired on NBC, 15 Jan. and 9 April 1998, respectively). There are also references to the murder of James Byrd Jr., a black man who was lynched by dragging in Jasper, Texas, on 7 June 1998; the Atlanta Child Murders, which occurred from 1979–1981; a string of Black and Brown girls who went missing in the D.C./Maryland area in March 2017, shortly before this poem was written; and the ongoing disappearances and murders of indigenous women in the U.S. and Canada.

"Pandemic": Toni Morrison's "Recitatif" is a short story about two women, Twyla and Roberta, who encounter each other for the first time as children in an orphanage, and then again and again throughout adulthood and middle age. While Twyla, the narrator, states that one of them is black and the other white, the specific racial identity of each character is unclear.

"Pickle Goddess": To view the video that inspired this poem, go to https://youtu .be/piG7lgtPKoY.

"and though the odds say improbable": The title of this poem is a lyric from Stevie Wonder's "Overjoyed," from the album *In Square Circle* (Tamla, 1985). The poem itself is written in the vein of E. E. cummings's "the Cambridge ladies who live in furnished souls," but follows a structure similar to Diane Seuss's "The famous poets came for us they came on us or some of us."